THUNDER

FOX'S

LONG

HAIR

(a true story)

Written by:
S. WILLIAM LONEWOLF

Illustrations by:
ADAM ROBERT DICK

Photos provided by:
MICHELLE GILLENWATER LALUMONDIER

AUTHORS DEDICATION:

To my daughters Beth and Kala for their unwavering support of my work. Thanks for putting up with me.

To my dearest friends Scott, Michelle, Anna (Spirit Pony) and of course Vincent (Thunder Fox). Without their love of family and friends this book would not have been possible.

THUNDER FOXES DEDICATION

To my Grandma Judy, you gave me the reason. To all the kids everywhere battling cancer and other diseases. "Never give up the fight."

AuthorHouse™
1663 Liberty Drive
Bloomington, IN 47403
www.authorhouse.com
Phone: 1-800-839-8640

Published by AuthorHouse 04/17/2012

ISBN: 978-1-4685-8095-2 (sc)

Library of Congress Control Number: 2012906444

Any people depicted in stock imagery provided by Thinkstock are models,
and such images are being used for illustrative purposes only.
Certain stock imagery © Thinkstock.

This book is printed on acid-free paper.

Because of the dynamic nature of the Internet, any web addresses or links contained in this book may have changed
since publication and may no longer be valid. The views expressed in this work are solely those of the author and do not
necessarily reflect the views of the publisher, and the publisher hereby disclaims any responsibility for them.

authorHOUSE®

THUNDER FOX'S

LONG HAIR

INSPIRED BY

A

TRUE STORY

At the very young age of ten a small Native American boy named Vincent Thunder Fox decided it was time to grow his hair long.

He wasn't quite sure why he wanted to do this, but being part Native American he knew that many of the boys and men of different Indian tribes wore their hair very long.

This was actually one of the steps that a young brave from many different tribes would take on his red road journey to becoming a great, powerful and wise warrior or chief.

Though young Thunder Fox of the Cherokee Wolf Clan did not know this at the time.

So from the age of ten on, young Thunder Fox did not cut his hair or let anyone else cut it for that matter. This made him very proud and happy.

Though as of yet he still was not quite sure why.

During this time Thunder Fox had to suffer through the many difficulties of having to deal with letting his hair grow to such a great length.

Many of these problems would have sent any number of boys running to a barber for relief.

Not Thunder Fox though. He had a purpose for growing his hair long. But so far he did not know what that was.

His mother and father did not object too much to Thunder Fox growing his hair so long. As long as he kept it neat, clean and combed. After all he was part Cherokee and this was a part of his heritage.

Almost every morning when Thunder Fox would wake up for school he would find his hair in a tangled up mess. One look in the mirror told him he was suffering from a nearly incurable case of bed head.

Some days Thunder Fox found this to be very funny and couldn't help but laugh at the way his hair was sticking up all over the place.

Other days it was downright scary when he looked in the mirror. Especially on the mornings when he would be running late for school.

Thunder Fox would not give up on his long hair though. He would just struggle to brush it out to make himself presentable before rushing off to school.

He still did not know why he went to all this trouble, but Thunder Fox was sure there was a very important reason.

One time when Thunder Fox was enjoying the day hanging out with some friends he started running to the top of a large hill.

On the way up he slipped and fell doing summersaults all the way back down to the bottom of the hill. His long black hair gathered up grass, sticks, leaves and even grasshoppers along the way.

The boy sat up dizzy and laughed along with his friends at the hilarious way his hair looked.

On many occasions at school he had to endure some teasing and name calling from several other boys that thought his long hair was silly and girlish. These bullies Thunder Fox ignored because they did not understand why he wanted his hair so long.

Come to think of it. He still wasn't quite sure why himself.

In the spring of his thirteenth year Thunder Fox's hair had grown to well over a foot long. It was at this time that he started truly learning about his Cherokee heritage from an elder named Lonewolf.

The Cherokee elder was very impressed with Thunder Fox and his long hair. It reminded him of the old ways of many Native American tribes.

As Spring turned into Summer it became unbearably hot for Thunder Fox because of his longhair. For the first time in many years he thought of cutting it off to gain some relief from the heat.

He told his teacher Lonewolf of his intentions.

Lonewolf was sympathetic to Thunder Fox's suffering. However he told his young student that because of the pride the boy felt for his heritage as well as his long hair, only he could make that decision.

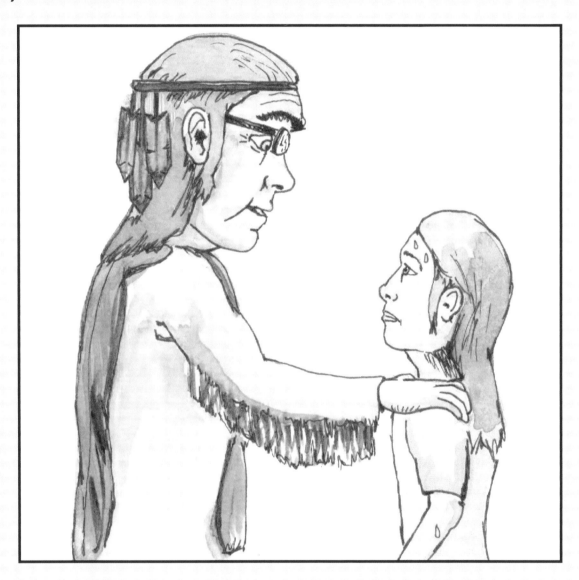

This was very troubling for Thunder Fox because though he was hot and miserable he still loved his long hair. However he still had not figured out why.

Luckily Thunder Fox's mother came to the rescue. She simply brushed his hair and put it into a long ponytail giving him much needed relief from the summers stifling weather.

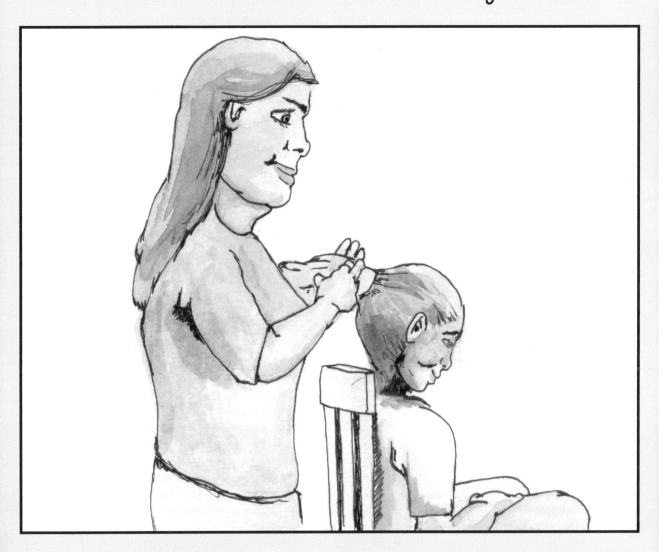

This made Thunder Fox very happy for now he could enjoy the warm summer days and not suffer with his long hair laying across his shoulders and neck.

It wasn't until the end of this long hot summer that Thunder Fox was able to attend his very first Pow Wow. A celebration of all Native American traditions. He along with his mother, father, little sister and his mother's friend met Lonewolf his teacher at the event.

Dressed in traditional Native American regalia, Thunder Fox was excited to be at his first Pow Wow, even though he was nervous about going into the circle to dance.

As the Pow Wow drum beat began Thunder Fox found himself enjoying the music and tapping his feet to the rhythm.

With the Pow Wow festivities under way, the elder Lonewolf invited Thunder Fox and his little sister Spirit Pony along with their father Four Eagles into the circle to dance. All of them had a great time as his mother recorded the event for their family history.

When Thunder Fox danced he let the spirit of the drum enter his heart. Doing this got him over being nervous and he danced with more joy and spirit than he had experienced at any other time in his young life.

This made him happy in many ways, though he was not sure yet what all of them were.

During one of the few dance breaks Thunder Fox overheard their friend talking to a Cherokee woman about her incredibly long hair.

The woman's hair was braided and nearly touched the ground.

As the young Cherokee boy listened, the woman told her story as to why she grew her hair so long.

She too was very proud of her hair and her Native American heritage, the woman told them.

But she also grew her hair long for another very important reason.

She grew it very long so that every year she could cut one or two feet of it off and donate it.

That was a strange thing to do Thunder Fox thought to himself. Who would want someone else's hair?

As the Pow Wow drum continued its beat and the festivities went on around him, Thunder Fox listened closer to what the woman had to say.

The Cherokee woman continued to explain. "I give a foot or two of my hair each year to an organization called Locks of Love so that it can be made into hairpieces for children that lose their hair due to various diseases and medical conditions"

That truly made so much sense to Thunder Fox. He had known people that had battled different diseases and had lost their hair. Including someone very close to him from his own family.

This got the young Cherokee boy thinking about his own long hair and why he grew it.

The Pow Wow continued on with more dancing, eating and craft buying for Thunder Fox and his family and friends.

As Thunder Fox continued to enjoy the day in the back of his mind he kept thinking of the Cherokee woman's words.

The Cherokee elder Lonewolf had a very long journey home and so they all decided it was time to leave the Pow Wow.

They said good bye to Lonewolf, and Thunder Fox, Spirit Pony, their mother, father and friend all headed for home as well.

During the ride home Thunder Fox was finally beginning to understand why he had grown his hair so long.

Several days past and Thunder Fox thought and thought about the Cherokee woman from the Pow Wow and what she had said about her long hair.

Finally he had made his decision on what he wanted to do. He talked to his mother about it and she set the whole thing up for him.

He then contacted Lonewolf to tell him about his plan.

"I've decided to get my hair cut", he told the elder Cherokee. "I want to donate it to Locks of Love so that a part of my heart will be with those children that have lost their own hair."

"I hope you understand my teacher. After all this is for a good cause."

Not only did Lonewolf understand, but he was incredibly proud of young Thunder Fox for his decision.

"You are performing a very noble and unselfish act my young Cherokee brother. For this you will always be considered a great warrior."

That very week Thunder Fox went to the barber and got his hair cut. His ponytail was fourteen inches long.

He immediately sent it to the Locks of Love organization so that as he had said....

"A part of my heart could go to help others."

Thunder Fox Before

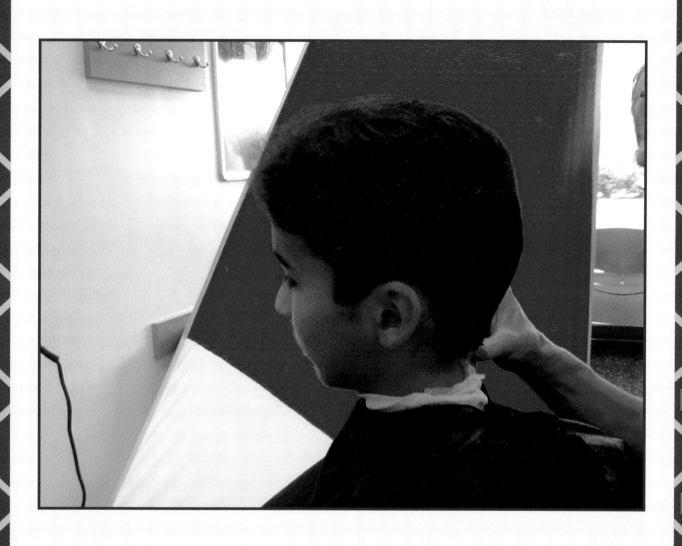

Thunder Fox After

THE END

For more information on

LOCKS OF LOVE

or if you wish to donate
contact:

LOCKS OF LOVE
234 SOUTHERN BLVD.
WEST PALM BEACH, FLORIDA
33405-2701
or call:
(561) 833-7332

Toll Free Information Line
(888) 896-1588
* * * * * * * *

WEBSITE:
www.locksoflove.org

E-MAIL
info@locksoflove.org

CPSIA information can be obtained at www.ICGtesting.com
Printed in the USA
LVIW01n0411141015
457986LV00005B/15